HORMONE RESET DIET

MEGA BUNDLE - 3 Manuscripts in 1 - 120+ Hormone Reset - friendly recipes including Side Dishes, Breakfast, and desserts for a delicious and tasty diet

TABLE OF CONTENTS

SIDE DISHES 9

FRIED VEGETABLES..... 9

ONION SAUCE 11

FISH "CAKE"..... 12

SUSHI HANDROLLS..... 13

STEAMED VEGETABLES 14

GUACAMOLE..... 15

CHICKEN NACHOS 16

SCRAMBLED EGGS WITH SALMON..... 17

CHICKEN WITH RICE 18

ROASTED VEGETABLES..... 19

SAUSAGE PIZZA 20

HEALTY PIZZA 21

SLAW 22

EDAMAME FRITATTA 23

ONION FRITATTA..... 24

LEAF FRITATTA 25

KALE FRITATTA 26

JICAMA FRITATTA..... 27

BROCCOLI FRITATTA..... 28

CAULIFLOWER SANDWICH 29

AVOCADO BOATS 30

MEXICAN CORN DIP 31

LEEK QUICHE 32

ROASTED SQUASH..... 34

BRUSSELS SPROUT CHIPS 35

CUCUMBER CHIPS 36

SQUASH CHIPS 37
PASTA..38
SIMPLE SPAGHETTI..38
SHRIMP PASTA 40
PASTA WITH OLIVES AND TOMATOES 41
SALAD..42
MORNING SALAD 42
TOMATO SOUP..43
CRAB SALAD 44
ASIAN SALAD 45
CHICKEN SALAD..46
CUCUMBER SALAD 47
GRAPEFRUIT SALAD..48
APPLE SALAD 49
COLESLAW..50
LOBSTER SALAD..51
RADISH SALAD..52
SPINACH SALAD..53
SECOND COOKBOOK..54
BREAKFAST 55
BEANS OMELETTE 55
ASIAN GREENS OMELETTE 56
BEANS OMELETTE 57
CABBAGE OMELETTE..58
MUSHROOM OMELETTE 59
TOMATO OMELETTE 60
OATS WITH PEANUT BUTTER 61
BREAKFAST GRANOLA..62

BANANA PANCAKES 63
LIME PANCAKES 64
GUAVA PANCAKES 65
APRICOT MUFFINS 66
PEACH MUFFINS....68
BLUEBERRY MUFFINS 69
PAPAYA MUFFINS....71
CORN OMELETTE....72
MUSHROOM OMELETTE 73
YAMS OMELETTE....74
RAISIN BREAKFAST MIX....75
SAUSAGE BREAKFAST SANDWICH....76
STRAWBERRY MUFFINS 77
LEEK FRITATTA....78
KALE FRITATTA 79
GREENS FRITATTA 80
BROCCOLI FRITATTA....81
DESSERTS 82
BREAKFAST COOKIES....82
BLUEBERRY PIE....84
PUMPKIN PIE....85
RICOTTA ICE-CREAM 86
SAFFRON ICE-CREAM 87
SMOOTHIES 88
TURMERIC-MANGO SMOOTHIE....88
AVOCADO-KALE SMOOTHIE....89
BUTTERMILK SMOOTHIE....90
GREEN SMOOTHIE....91

FRUIT SMOOTHIE 92
MANGO SMOOTHIE 93
DREAMSICLE SMOOTHIE 94
FIG SMOOTHIE 95
POMEGRANATE SMOOTHIE 96
GINGER-KALE SMOOTHIE 97
THIRD COOKBOOK 98
BREAKFAST 99
PINEAPPLE PANCAKES 99
ALMOND PANCAKES 100
APPLE PANCAKES 101
STRAWBERRY PANCAKES 102
PEAR PANCAKES 103
LETTUCE OMELETTE 104
ZUCCHINI OMELETTE 105
JICAMA OMELETTE 106
MUSHROOM OMELETTE 107
BASIL OMELETTE 108
MUSHROOM OMELETTE 109
BREAKFAST MIX 110
SAUSAGE BREAKFAST SANDWICH 111
BREAKFAST GRANOLA 112
PANCAKES 113
BANANA PANCAKES 113
PINEAPPLE PANCAKES 114
ALMOND PANCAKES 115
APPLE PANCAKES 116
STRAWBERRY PANCAKES 117

PEAR PANCAKES....118

COOKIES....119

BREAKFAST COOKIES....119

SMOOOTHIES....120

FIG SMOOTHIE....120

POMEGRANATE SMOOTHIE....121

GINGER-KALE SMOOTHIE....122

BERRY YOGHURT SMOOTHIE....123

COCONUT SMOOTHIE....124

RASPBERRY-VANILLA SMOOTHIE....125

CHERRY SMOOTHIE....126

CHOCOLATE SMOOTHIE....127

TOFU SMOOTHIE....128

ORANGE SMOOTHIE....129

RAISIN DATE SMOOTHIE....130

MUFFINS....131

SIMPLE MUFFINS....131

GINGERBREAD MUFFINS....133

CHERRIES MUFFINS....135

BLUEBERRY MUFFINS....136

BERRIES MUFFINS....137

CHOCOLATE MUFFINS....138

RASPBERRIES MUFFINS....139

Introduction

Hormone Reset recipes for personal enjoyment but also for family enjoyment. You will love them for sure for how easy it is to prepare them.

SIDE DISHES

FRIED VEGETABLES

Serves: 2

Prep Time: *10* Minutes

Cook Time: *15* Minutes

Total Time: *25* Minutes

INGREDIENTS

- **1 cup red bell pepper**
- **¼ cup cucumber**
- **¼ cup zucchini**
- **¼ cup asparagus**
- **¼ cup carrots**
- **1 onion**
- **2 eggs**
- **1 tsp salt**
- **1 tsp pepper**
- **Seasoning**
- **1 tablespoon olive oil**

DIRECTIONS

1. **In a skillet heat olive oil and sauté onion until soft**
2. **Chop vegetables into thin slices and pour over onion**

3. Whisk eggs with salt and pepper and pour over the vegetables
4. Cook until vegetables are brown
5. When ready remove from heat and serve

ONION SAUCE

Serves: *4*

Prep Time: *10* Minutes

Cook Time: *55* Minutes

Total Time: *65* Minutes

INGREDIENTS

- 1 onion
- 2 garlic cloves
- ¼ lb. carrots
- 1 potato
- 1 tablespoon balsamic vinegar
- ¼ tsp salt
- ¼ tsp black pepper
- 1 tablespoon olive oil
- 1 cup water

DIRECTIONS

1. Chop all the vegetables and place them in a heated skillet
2. Add remaining ingredients and cook on low heat
3. Allow to simmer for 40-45 minutes or until vegetables are soft
4. Transfer mixture to a blender and blend until smooth
5. When ready remove from the blender and serve

FISH "CAKE"

Serves: ***4-6***

Prep Time: ***10*** Minutes

Cook Time: ***50*** Minutes

Total Time: ***60*** Minutes

INGREDIENTS

- 2 tuna tins
- 2 potatoes
- 2 eggs
- 1 handful of gluten free flour
- 1 handful of parsley
- black pepper
- 1 cup breadcrumbs

DIRECTIONS

1. **Preheat the oven to 350 F**
2. **Boil the potatoes until they are soft**
3. **Mix the tuna with parsley, black pepper and salt**
4. **Roll fish into patties and dip into a bowl with flour, then eggs and then breadcrumbs**
5. **Place the patties on a baking tray**
6. **Bake at 350 F for 40-45 minutes**
7. **When ready remove from heat and serve**

SUSHI HANDROLLS

Serves: 2

Prep Time: *10* Minutes

Cook Time: *25* Minutes

Total Time: *35* Minutes

INGREDIENTS

- 1 sushi nori packet
- 4 tablespoons mayonnaise
- ½ lb. smoked salmon
- 1 tsp wasabi
- 1 cup cooked sushi rice
- 1 avocado

DIRECTIONS

1. **Cut avocado and into thin slices**
2. **Take a sheet of sushi and spread mayonnaise onto the sheet**
3. **Add rice, salmon and avocado**
4. **Roll and dip sushi into wasabi and serve**

STEAMED VEGETABLES

Serves: 2
Prep Time: *10* Minutes

Cook Time: *10* Minutes

Total Time: *20* Minutes

INGREDIENTS

- **1 carrot**
- **2 sweet potato**
- **2 parsnips**
- **1 zucchini**
- **2 broccoli stems**

DIRECTIONS

1. **Chop vegetables into thin slices**
2. **Place all the vegetables into a steamer**
3. **Add enough water and cook on high until vegetables are steamed**
4. **When ready remove from the steamer and serve**

GUACAMOLE

Serves: 2

Prep Time: 5 Minutes

Cook Time: 5 Minutes

Total Time: *10* Minutes

INGREDIENTS

- 1 avocado
- 1 lime juice
- 1 handful of coriander
- 1 tsp olive oil
- 1 tsp salt
- 1 tsp pepper

DIRECTIONS

1. **Place all the ingredients in a blender**
2. **Blend until smooth and transfer to a bowl**

CHICKEN NACHOS

Serves: ***4-6***

Prep Time: *15* Minutes

Cook Time: *35* Minutes

Total Time: *50* Minutes

INGREDIENTS

- **2 chicken breasts**
- **Tortilla chips**
- **Fajita seasoning**
- **¼ cup cheddar cheese**
- **4-5 mushrooms**
- **Guacamole**
- **¼ cup peppers**

DIRECTIONS

1. **In a pan heat olive oil and add chopped onion, sauté until soft**
2. **Add chicken, fajita seasoning and remaining vegetables**
3. **Cook on low heat for 10-12 minutes**
4. **Place tortilla chips into a baking dish, sprinkle cheese and bake in the oven until cheese has melted**
5. **Remove from the oven pour sautéed vegetables and chicken over and tortilla chips and serve**

SCRAMBLED EGGS WITH SALMON

Serves: 2
Prep Time: *10* Minutes

Cook Time: *20* Minutes

Total Time: *30* Minutes

INGREDIENTS

- ½ lb. smoked salmon
- 2 eggs
- 1 avocado
- 1 tsp salt
- 1 tsp pepper
- 1 tps olive oil

DIRECTIONS

1. **In a bowl whisk the eggs with salt and pepper**
2. **In a skillet heat olive oil and pour the egg mixture**
3. **Add salmon pieces to the mixture and cook for 2-3 minutes per side**
4. **When ready remove from the skillet, add avocado and serve**

CHICKEN WITH RICE

Serves: *4*

Prep Time: *10* Minutes

Cook Time: *25* Minutes

Total Time: *35* Minutes

INGREDIENTS

- 2 chicken breasts
- 1 cup cooked white rice
- 2 tablespoons mayonnaise
- 1 tablespoon curry powder
- 1 zucchini
- 1 cup broccoli
- 1 tablespoon olive oil

DIRECTIONS

1. Cut chicken breast into small pieces and set aside
2. In a pan heat olive oil and cook the chicken breast for 4-5 minutes
3. In another bowl combine mayonnaise, curry powder and add mixture to the chicken
4. Add remaining ingredients and cook for another 10-12 minutes or until the chicken is ready
5. When ready remove from the pot and serve with white rice

ROASTED VEGETABLES

Serves: 2

Prep Time: *10* Minutes

Cook Time: *50* Minutes

Total Time: *60* Minutes

INGREDIENTS

- 1 carrot
- 2 sweet potatoes
- 1 butternut squash
- 2 parsnips
- 1 rosemary spring
- 2 bay leaves

DIRECTIONS

1. Chop the vegetables into thin slices
2. Place everything in a prepare baking dish
3. Bake at 350 F for 40-45 minutes or until vegetables are golden brown
4. When ready remove from the oven and serve

SAUSAGE PIZZA

Serves: *6-8*

Prep Time: *10* Minutes

Cook Time: *15* Minutes

Total Time: *25* Minutes

INGREDIENTS

- **2 pork sausages**
- **1 tablespoon olive oil**
- **2 garlic cloves**
- **1 tsp fennel seeds**
- **½ lb. ricotta**
- **1 cup mozzarella cheese**
- **1 oz. parmesan cheese**
- **1 pizza crust**

DIRECTIONS

1. **Spread tomato sauce on the pizza crust**
2. **Place all the toppings on the pizza crust**
3. **Bake the pizza at 425 F for 12-15 minutes**
4. **When ready remove pizza from the oven and serve**

HEALTY PIZZA

Serves: *6-8*

Prep Time: *10* Minutes

Cook Time: *15* Minutes

Total Time: 25 Minutes

INGREDIENTS

- 1 pizza crust
- 1 tablespoon olive oil
- 1 garlic clove
- 1 cup tomatoes
- 1 cup mozzarella cheese
- 1 carrot
- 1 cucumber

DIRECTIONS

1. **Spread tomato sauce on the pizza crust**
2. **Place all the toppings on the pizza crust**
3. **Bake the pizza at 425 F for 12-15 minutes**
4. **When ready remove pizza from the oven and serve**

SLAW

Serves: *1*

Prep Time: *5* Minutes

Cook Time: *5* Minutes

Total Time: ***10*** Minutes

INGREDIENTS

- **1 cabbage**
- **1 bunch of baby carrots**
- **½ cucumber**
- **1 bun of cilantro**
- **1 bunch of basil**
- **1 onion**

DIRECTIONS

1. **In a bowl combine all ingredients together and mix well**
2. **Serve with dressing**

EDAMAME FRITATTA

Serves: 2

Prep Time: *10* Minutes

Cook Time: *20* Minutes

Total Time: *30* Minutes

INGREDIENTS

- 1 cup edamame
- 1 tablespoon olive oil
- ½ red onion
- 2 eggs
- ¼ tsp salt
- 2 oz. cheddar cheese
- 1 garlic clove
- ¼ tsp dill

DIRECTIONS

1. **In a bowl whisk eggs with salt and cheese**
2. **In a frying pan heat olive oil and pour egg mixture**
3. **Add remaining ingredients and mix well**
4. **Serve when ready**

ONION FRITATTA

Serves: 2

Prep Time: *10* Minutes

Cook Time: *20* Minutes

Total Time: *30* Minutes

INGREDIENTS

- **1 tablespoon olive oil**
- **½ red onion**
- **2 eggs**
- **¼ tsp salt**
- **2 oz. cheddar cheese**
- **1 garlic clove**
- **¼ tsp dill**

DIRECTIONS

1. **In a bowl whisk eggs with salt and cheese**
2. **In a frying pan heat olive oil and pour egg mixture**
3. **Add remaining ingredients and mix well**
4. **Serve when ready**

LEAF FRITATTA

Serves: 2
Prep Time: *10* Minutes

Cook Time: *20* Minutes

Total Time: *30* Minutes

INGREDIENTS

- ½ lb. leaf
- 1 tablespoon olive oil
- ½ red onion
- 2 eggs
- ¼ tsp salt
- 2 oz. cheddar cheese
- 1 garlic clove
- ¼ tsp dill

DIRECTIONS

1. **In a bowl whisk eggs with salt and cheese**
2. **In a frying pan heat olive oil and pour egg mixture**
3. **Add remaining ingredients and mix well**
4. **Serve when ready**

KALE FRITATTA

Serves: 2
Prep Time: *10* Minutes
Cook Time: *20* Minutes
Total Time: *30* Minutes

INGREDIENTS

- **1 cup kale**
- **1 tablespoon olive oil**
- **½ red onion**
- **2 eggs**
- **¼ tsp salt**
- **2 oz. cheddar cheese**
- **1 garlic clove**
- **¼ tsp dill**

DIRECTIONS

1. **In a skillet sauté kale until tender**
2. **In a bowl whisk eggs with salt and cheese**
3. **In a frying pan heat olive oil and pour egg mixture**
4. **Add remaining ingredients and mix well**
5. **When ready serve with sautéed kale**

JICAMA FRITATTA

Serves: 2

Prep Time: *10* Minutes

Cook Time: *20* Minutes

Total Time: *30* Minutes

INGREDIENTS

- ½ cup jicama
- 1 tablespoon olive oil
- ½ red onion
- 2 eggs
- ¼ tsp salt
- 2 oz. parmesan cheese
- 1 garlic clove
- ¼ tsp dill

DIRECTIONS

1. **In a bowl whisk eggs with salt and parmesan cheese**
2. **In a frying pan heat olive oil and pour egg mixture**
3. **Add remaining ingredients and mix well**
4. **Serve when ready**

BROCCOLI FRITATTA

Serves: 2
Prep Time: *10* Minutes

Cook Time: *20* Minutes

Total Time: *30* Minutes

INGREDIENTS

- **1 cup broccoli**
- **1 tablespoon olive oil**
- **½ red onion**
- **2 eggs**
- **¼ tsp salt**
- **2 oz. cheddar cheese**
- **1 garlic clove**
- **¼ tsp dill**

DIRECTIONS

1. **In a skillet sauté broccoli until tender**
2. **In a bowl whisk eggs with salt and cheese**
3. **In a frying pan heat olive oil and pour egg mixture**
4. **Add remaining ingredients and mix well**
5. **When ready serve with sautéed broccoli**

CAULIFLOWER SANDWICH

Serves: 2

Prep Time: *10* Minutes

Cook Time: *30* Minutes

Total Time: *40* Minutes

INGREDIENTS

- 1 head cauliflower
- 4 tablespoons olive oil
- ¼ tsp salt
- ½ red onion
- 2 tablespoons tahini
- 1 clove garlic
- 4 slices gluten-free bread
- 1 avocado

DIRECTIONS

1. Toss the cauliflower with olive oil and roast at 400 F for 22-25 minutes
2. In a saucepan sauté the onion until soft
3. Add roasted cauliflower, tahini, olive oil, salt and cook for 1-2 minutes
4. Place everything in a blender and blend until smooth
5. Spread mixture over bread slices

AVOCADO BOATS

Serves: 2

Prep Time: *10* Minutes

Cook Time: *10* Minutes

Total Time: *20* Minutes

INGREDIENTS

- **1 can chickpeas**
- **¼ red onion**
- **¼ tsp turmeric**
- **1 tablespoon dill**
- **½ tsp garlic powder**
- **1 tablespoon mustard**
- **½ cup tahini**
- **2 avocados**

DIRECTIONS

1. **Cut avocado in half and scoop out part of the interior**
2. **In a bowl combine together chickpeas with onion, turmeric, dill, garlic, tahini and mustard**
3. **Mix well and spoon mixture into avocado halves**
4. **Serve when ready**

MEXICAN CORN DIP

Serves: 2

Prep Time: *10* Minutes

Cook Time: *20* Minutes

Total Time: *30* Minutes

INGREDIENTS

- 2 cups kernels
- 1 tablespoon butter
- 1 jalapeno pepper
- 1 tsp chili powder
- 1 red onion
- ½ cup mayonnaise
- 1 tablespoon lime juice
- 2 tablespoons cilantro

DIRECTIONS

1. **In a skillet melt butter over medium heat**
2. **Add corn and cook for 5-6 minutes**
3. **Add chili powder, jalapeno, red onion and cook on low heat**
4. **Add lime juice, mayonnaise and cook for another 2-3 minutes**
5. **Remove from heat, stir in cilantro and serve with tortilla chips**

LEEK QUICHE

Serves: *4*

Prep Time: *10* Minutes

Cook Time: *50* Minutes

Total Time: *60* Minutes

INGREDIENTS

- 1 tablespoon butter
- 1 bunch asparagus
- 1 leek
- ¼ tsp salt
- 2 eggs
- ½ cup vanilla yogurt
- 1 cup almond milk
- 1 cup cheese
- 1 pie crust

DIRECTIONS

1. In a saucepan melt butter, add leek, asparagus, pepper, salt and cook until vegetables are soft
2. In a bowl combine eggs, milk, yogurt and mix well
3. Place egg mixture on the pie crust
4. Top with asparagus and leek
5. Bake at 375 F for 40-45 minutes

6. **When ready remove from the oven and serve**

ROASTED SQUASH

Serves:	*3-4*	
Prep Time:	*10*	Minutes
Cook Time:	*20*	Minutes
Total Time:	*30*	Minutes

INGREDIENTS

- **2 delicata squashes**
- **2 tablespoons olive oil**
- **1 tsp curry powder**
- **1 tsp salt**

DIRECTIONS

1. **Preheat the oven to 400 F**
2. **Cut everything in half lengthwise**
3. **Toss everything with olive oil and place onto a prepared baking sheet**
4. **Roast for 18-20 minutes at 400 F or until golden brown**
5. **When ready remove from the oven and serve**

BRUSSELS SPROUT CHIPS

Serves: *2*
Prep Time: *10* Minutes

Cook Time: *20* Minutes

Total Time: *30* Minutes

INGREDIENTS

- 1 lb. brussels sprouts
- 1 tablespoon olive oil
- 1 tablespoon parmesan cheese
- 1 tsp garlic powder
- 1 tsp seasoning

DIRECTIONS

1. Preheat the oven to 425 F
2. In a bowl toss everything with olive oil and seasoning
3. Spread everything onto a prepared baking sheet
4. Bake for 8-10 minutes or until crisp
5. When ready remove from the oven and serve

CUCUMBER CHIPS

Serves: 2

Prep Time: *10* Minutes

Cook Time: *20* Minutes

Total Time: *30* Minutes

INGREDIENTS

- **1 lb. cucumber**
- **1 tsp salt**
- **1 tsp smoked paprika**
- **1 tablespoon olive oil**

DIRECTIONS

1. **Preheat the oven to 425 F**
2. **In a bowl toss everything with olive oil and seasoning**
3. **Spread everything onto a prepared baking sheet**
4. **Bake for 8-10 minutes or until crisp**
5. **When ready remove from the oven and serve**

SQUASH CHIPS

Serves: 2

Prep Time: *10* Minutes

Cook Time: *20* Minutes

Total Time: *30* Minutes

INGREDIENTS

- 1 lb. squash
- 1 tsp salt
- 1 tsp smoked paprika
- 1 tablespoon olive oil

DIRECTIONS

1. **Preheat the oven to 425 F**
2. **In a bowl toss everything with olive oil and seasoning**
3. **Spread everything onto a prepared baking sheet**
4. **Bake for 8-10 minutes or until crisp**
5. **When ready remove from the oven and serve**

PASTA

SIMPLE SPAGHETTI

Serves: 2
Prep Time: *5* Minutes

Cook Time: *15* Minutes

Total Time: *20* Minutes

INGREDIENTS

- **10 oz. spaghetti**
- **2 eggs**
- **½ cup parmesan cheese**
- **1 tsp black pepper**
- **Olive oil**
- **1 tsp parsley**
- **2 cloves garlic**

DIRECTIONS

1. **In a pot boil spaghetti (or any other type of pasta), drain and set aside**
2. **In a bowl whish eggs with parmesan cheese**
3. **In a skillet heat olive oil, add garlic and cook for 1-2 minutes**
4. **Pour egg mixture and mix well**
5. **Add pasta and stir well**

6. **When ready garnish with parsley and serve**

SHRIMP PASTA

Serves: 2

Prep Time: 5 Minutes

Cook Time: *15* Minutes

Total Time: *20* Minutes

INGREDIENTS

- **¼ cup mayonnaise**
- **¼ cup sweet chili sauce**
- **1 tablespoon lime juice**
- **1 garlic clove**
- **8 z. pasta**
- **1 lb. shrimp**
- **¼ tsp paprika**

DIRECTIONS

1. **In a pot boil spaghetti (or any other type of pasta), drain and set aside**
2. **Place all the ingredients for the sauce in a pot and bring to a simmer**
3. **Add pasta and mix well**
4. **When ready garnish with parmesan cheese and serve**

PASTA WITH OLIVES AND TOMATOES

Serves: 2

Prep Time: *5* Minutes

Cook Time: *15* Minutes

Total Time: *20* Minutes

INGREDIENTS

- 8 oz. pasta
- 3 tablespoons olive oil
- 2 cloves garlic
- 5-6 anchovy fillets
- 2 cups tomatoes
- 1 cup olives
- ½ cup basil leaves

DIRECTIONS

1. **In a pot boil spaghetti (or any other type of pasta), drain and set aside**
2. **Place all the ingredients for the sauce in a pot and bring to a simmer**
3. **Add pasta and mix well**
4. **When ready garnish with parmesan cheese and serve**

SALAD

MORNING SALAD

Serves: 2
Prep Time: 5 Minutes

Cook Time: 5 Minutes

Total Time: *10* Minutes

INGREDIENTS

- **1 onion**
- **1 tsp cumin**
- **1 tablespoon olive oil**
- **1 avocado**
- **¼ lb. cooked lentils**
- **1 oz. walnuts**
- **Coriander**
- **¼ lb. feta cheese**
- **Salad dressing of choice**
- **8-10 baby carrots**

DIRECTIONS

1. **In a bowl combine all ingredients together and mix well**
2. **Add dressing and serve**

TOMATO SOUP

Serves: *1*

Prep Time: *5* Minutes

Cook Time: *10* Minutes

Total Time: *15* Minutes

INGREDIENTS

- ¾ cup chicken broth
- 2 tbs tomato paste
- 2 tbs milk
- ½ cup tomatoes
- 1 tbs vinegar
- 1 tbs onion
- 1 clove garlic
- 1 tsp oregano
- Salt
- Pepper
- Basil leaves

DIRECTIONS

1. Pulse the ingredients in a food processor, saving the basil for garnish.
2. Cook the mixture until heated.
3. Serve garnished with basil leaves and toast.

CRAB SALAD

Serves: *1*
Prep Time: *5* Minutes
Cook Time: *10* Minutes
Total Time: *15* Minutes

INGREDIENTS

- ½ cup celery
- 1 tbs vinegar
- 1 tsp seasoning
- 100 g crab
- Red pepper flakes
- 2 tbs lemon juice
- 2 tbs onion

DIRECTIONS

1. Sauté the ingredients in a pan until celery is tender.
2. Season to taste.
3. Serve when ready

ASIAN SALAD

Serves: *1*
Prep Time: *5* Minutes

Cook Time: *5* Minutes

Total Time: ***10*** Minutes

INGREDIENTS

- **½ cup orange segments**
- **1 packet stevia**
- **1 toast**
- **100g chicken breast**
- **¼ tsp salt**
- **Orange citrus dressing**
- **2 cups romaine lettuce**

DIRECTIONS

1. **Cook the chicken in a skillet until golden.**
2. **Combine all of the ingredients in a bowl.**
3. **Serve immediately.**

CHICKEN SALAD

Serves: *1*

Prep Time: *5* Minutes

Cook Time: *10* Minutes

Total Time: *15* Minutes

INGREDIENTS

- 100g chicken
- ½ tsp onion powder
- ½ tsp garlic powder
- ½ tsp oregano
- 1 tsp paprika
- ½ tsp thyme
- ½ tsp black pepper
- ¼ tsp salad greens

DIRECTIONS

1. Rub the chicken with the combined spices.
2. Grill the pink until golden.
3. Serve over the salad greens and desired dressing.

CUCUMBER SALAD

Serves: *1*

Prep Time: *5* Minutes

Cook Time: *0* Minutes

Total Time: *5* Minutes

INGREDIENTS

- ¼ tsp salt
- 2 tsp parsley
- ¼ cup vinegar
- 2 tsp green onion
- Pepper
- Stevia
- 1 cucumber

DIRECTIONS

1. **Chop the cucumber.**
2. **Mix the ingredients in a bowl.**
3. **Refrigerate for at least 10 minutes, then serve.**

GRAPEFRUIT SALAD

Serves: *1*

Prep Time: *10* Minutes

Cook Time: *0* Minutes

Total Time: *10* Minutes

INGREDIENTS

- 2 tbs apple vinegar
- Grapefruit juice
- ½ tsp ginger
- Salt
- 1 red grapefruit
- 1 cucumber
- Pepper
- Cilantro
- 2 tbs onion
- Ruby red dressing

DIRECTIONS

1. **Peel the grapefruit and cut it into cubes.**
2. **Mix with the rest of the ingredients and season.**
3. **Serve topped with red dressing.**

APPLE SALAD

Serves: 2
Prep Time: 5 Minutes

Cook Time: *0* Minutes

Total Time: 5 Minutes

INGREDIENTS

- ½ cup green apple
- 1 tbs lemon juice
- Salt
- Pepper
- Stevia
- ½ cup cucumber
- 2 tbs apple cider vinegar

DIRECTIONS

1. **Chop the apple and cucumber.**
2. **Combine the ingredients and add stevia.**
3. **Serve immediately.**

COLESLAW

Serves: *1*

Prep Time: *10* Minutes

Cook Time: *0* Minutes

Total Time: *10* Minutes

INGREDIENTS

- **1 ½ cups cabbage**
- **¼ tsp onion powder**
- **Cayenne pepper**
- **Salt**
- **Pepper**
- **2 tbs vinegar**
- **2 tbs lemon juice**
- **1 tsp horseradish**
- **1 clove garlic**
- **½ tsp mustard**

DIRECTIONS

1. **Slice the cabbage.**
2. **Mix the rest of the ingredients in a bowl.**
3. **Pour the mixture over the cabbage and serve.**

LOBSTER SALAD

Serves: *1*

Prep Time: 5 Minutes

Cook Time: 5 Minutes

Total Time: *10* Minutes

INGREDIENTS

- 100g lobster
- 1 serving Tarragon Vinaigrette
- 2 tbs lemon juice
- 1 tbs tarragon
- ½ tsp garlic powder
- 2 tbs onion
- 1 tbs green onion

DIRECTIONS

1. **Cook the lobster.**
2. **Sauté the lobster, lemon juice, green onion, onion, tarragon, garlic powder, salt, and pepper until onion is tender.**
3. **Top the lettuce with the lobster mixture.**
4. **Serve topped with Tarragon Vinaigrette.**

RADISH SALAD

Serves: *1*

Prep Time: *10* Minutes

Cook Time: *20* Minutes

Total Time: *30* Minutes

INGREDIENTS

- **2 tbs lemon juice**
- **1 tbs onion**
- **1 tbs parsley**
- **Salt**
- **Radishes**
- **Pepper**

DIRECTIONS

1. **Combine all of the ingredients in a bowl.**
2. **Refrigerate for at least 20 minutes.**
3. **Serve.**

SPINACH SALAD

Serves: 1
Prep Time: 5 Minutes

Cook Time: 5 Minutes

Total Time: 10 Minutes

INGREDIENTS

- 1 bunch spinach
- Pepper
- Mint leaves
- 2 tbs vinegar
- 2 tbs lemon juice
- 5 strawberries
- ¼ tsp Stevia
- Salt

DIRECTIONS

1. Blend 2 strawberries, lemon juice, vinegar, Stevia, salt, and pepper together.
2. Pour the dressing over the salad and the sliced remained strawberry.
3. Serve topped with mint leaves.

SECOND COOKBOOK

BEANS OMELETTE

Serves: *1*
Prep Time: *5* Minutes

Cook Time: *10* Minutes

Total Time: *15* Minutes

INGREDIENTS

- **2 eggs**
- **¼ tsp salt**
- **¼ tsp black pepper**
- **1 tablespoon olive oil**
- **¼ cup cheese**
- **¼ tsp basil**
- **1 cup beans**

DIRECTIONS

1. **In a bowl combine all ingredients together and mix well**
2. **In a skillet heat olive oil and pour the egg mixture**
3. **Cook for 1-2 minutes per side**
4. **When ready remove omelette from the skillet and serve**

ASIAN GREENS OMELETTE

Serves: *1*

Prep Time: *5* Minutes

Cook Time: *10* Minutes

Total Time: *15* Minutes

INGREDIENTS

- **2 eggs**
- **¼ tsp salt**
- **¼ tsp black pepper**
- **1 tablespoon olive oil**
- **¼ cup cheese**
- **¼ tsp basil**
- **1 cup Asian greens**

DIRECTIONS

1. **In a bowl combine all ingredients together and mix well**
2. **In a skillet heat olive oil and pour the egg mixture**
3. **Cook for 1-2 minutes per side**
4. **When ready remove omelette from the skillet and serve**

BEANS OMELETTE

Serves: *1*
Prep Time: *5* Minutes

Cook Time: *10* Minutes

Total Time: *15* Minutes

INGREDIENTS

- **2 eggs**
- **¼ tsp salt**
- **¼ tsp black pepper**
- **1 tablespoon olive oil**
- **¼ cup cheese**
- **¼ tsp basil**
- **1 cup beans**

DIRECTIONS

1. **In a bowl combine all ingredients together and mix well**
2. **In a skillet heat olive oil and pour the egg mixture**
3. **Cook for 1-2 minutes per side**
4. **When ready remove omelette from the skillet and serve**

CABBAGE OMELETTE

Serves: *1*

Prep Time: *5* Minutes

Cook Time: *10* Minutes

Total Time: *15* Minutes

INGREDIENTS

- **2 eggs**
- **¼ tsp salt**
- **¼ tsp black pepper**
- **1 tablespoon olive oil**
- **¼ cup cheese**
- **¼ tsp basil**
- **1 cup red onion**
- **1 cup cabbage**

DIRECTIONS

1. **In a bowl combine all ingredients together and mix well**
2. **In a skillet heat olive oil and pour the egg mixture**
3. **Cook for 1-2 minutes per side**
4. **When ready remove omelette from the skillet and serve**

MUSHROOM OMELETTE

Serves: *1*

Prep Time: *5* Minutes

Cook Time: *10* Minutes

Total Time: *15* Minutes

INGREDIENTS

- 2 eggs
- ¼ tsp salt
- ¼ tsp black pepper
- 1 tablespoon olive oil
- ¼ cup cheese
- ¼ tsp basil
- 1 cup mushrooms

DIRECTIONS

1. **In a bowl combine all ingredients together and mix well**
2. **In a skillet heat olive oil and pour the egg mixture**
3. **Cook for 1-2 minutes per side**
4. **When ready remove omelette from the skillet and serve**

TOMATO OMELETTE

Serves: *1*

Prep Time: *5* Minutes

Cook Time: *10* Minutes

Total Time: *15* Minutes

INGREDIENTS

- **2 eggs**
- **¼ tsp salt**
- **¼ tsp black pepper**
- **1 tablespoon olive oil**
- **¼ cup cheese**
- **¼ tsp basil**
- **1 cup tomatoes**

DIRECTIONS

1. **In a bowl combine all ingredients together and mix well**
2. **In a skillet heat olive oil and pour the egg mixture**
3. **Cook for 1-2 minutes per side**
4. **When ready remove omelette from the skillet and serve**

OATS WITH PEANUT BUTTER

Serves: *1*

Prep Time: *5* Minutes

Cook Time: *5* Minutes

Total Time: ***10*** Minutes

INGREDIENTS

- 1 cup oats
- 3 tablespoons peanut butter
- ½ cup almond milk
- ¼ banana

DIRECTIONS

1. **In a bowl combine all ingredients together and mix well**
2. **Pour mixture into a jar**
3. **Refrigerate overnight**
4. **Serve in the morning**

BREAKFAST GRANOLA

Serves: 2

Prep Time: *5* Minutes

Cook Time: *30* Minutes

Total Time: *35* Minutes

INGREDIENTS

- 1 tsp vanilla extract
- 1 tablespoon honey
- 1 lb. rolled oats
- 2 tablespoons sesame seeds
- ¼ lb. almonds
- ¼ lb. berries

DIRECTIONS

1. Preheat the oven to 325 F
2. Spread the granola onto a baking sheet
3. Bake for 12-15 minutes, remove and mix everything
4. Bake for another 12-15 minutes or until slightly brown
5. When ready remove from the oven and serve

BANANA PANCAKES

Serves: ***4***

Prep Time: ***10*** Minutes

Cook Time: ***20*** Minutes

Total Time: ***30*** Minutes

INGREDIENTS

- **1 cup whole wheat flour**
- **¼ tsp baking soda**
- **¼ tsp baking powder**
- **1 cup mashed banana**
- **2 eggs**
- **1 cup milk**

DIRECTIONS

1. **In a bowl combine all ingredients together and mix well**
2. **In a skillet heat olive oil**
3. **Pour ¼ of the batter and cook each pancake for 1-2 minutes per side**
4. **When ready remove from heat and serve**

LIME PANCAKES

Serves: *4*

Prep Time: *10* Minutes

Cook Time: *20* Minutes

Total Time: *30* Minutes

INGREDIENTS

- 1 cup whole wheat flour
- ¼ tsp baking soda
- ¼ tsp baking powder
- 1 cup lime
- 2 eggs
- 1 cup milk

DIRECTIONS

1. In a bowl combine all ingredients together and mix well
2. In a skillet heat olive oil
3. Pour ¼ of the batter and cook each pancake for 1-2 minutes per side
4. When ready remove from heat and serve

GUAVA PANCAKES

Serves: *4*

Prep Time: *10* Minutes

Cook Time: *30* Minutes

Total Time: *40* Minutes

INGREDIENTS

- 1 cup whole wheat flour
- ¼ tsp baking soda
- ¼ tsp baking powder
- 2 eggs
- 1 cup milk
- 1 cup guava

DIRECTIONS

1. In a bowl combine all ingredients together and mix well
2. In a skillet heat olive oil
3. Pour ¼ of the batter and cook each pancake for 1-2 minutes per side
4. When ready remove from heat and serve

APRICOT MUFFINS

Serves: *8-12*

Prep Time: ***10*** Minutes

Cook Time: ***20*** Minutes

Total Time: ***30*** Minutes

INGREDIENTS

- **2 eggs**
- **1 tablespoon olive oil**
- **1 cup milk**
- **2 cups whole wheat flour**
- **1 tsp baking soda**
- **¼ tsp baking soda**
- **1 tsp ginger**
- **1 cup apricot**
- **¼ cup molasses**

DIRECTIONS

1. **In a bowl combine all dry ingredients**
2. **In another bowl combine all dry ingredients**
3. **Combine wet and dry ingredients together**
4. **Pour mixture into 8-12 prepared muffin cups, fill 2/3 of the cups**
5. **Bake for 18-20 minutes at 375 F**

6. **When ready remove from the oven and serve**

PEACH MUFFINS

Serves: *8-12*

Prep Time: ***10*** Minutes

Cook Time: ***20*** Minutes

Total Time: ***30*** Minutes

INGREDIENTS

- 2 eggs
- 1 tablespoon olive oil
- 1 cup milk
- 2 cups whole wheat flour
- 1 tsp baking soda
- ¼ tsp baking soda
- 1 tsp cinnamon
- 1 cup mashed peaches

DIRECTIONS

1. In a bowl combine all dry ingredients
2. In another bowl combine all dry ingredients
3. Combine wet and dry ingredients together
4. Pour mixture into 8-12 prepared muffin cups, fill 2/3 of the cups
5. Bake for 18-20 minutes at 375 F
6. When ready remove from the oven and serve

BLUEBERRY MUFFINS

Serves: *8-12*
Prep Time: *10* Minutes

Cook Time: *20* Minutes

Total Time: *30* Minutes

INGREDIENTS

- 2 eggs
- 1 tablespoon olive oil
- 1 cup milk
- 2 cups whole wheat flour
- 1 tsp baking soda
- ¼ tsp baking soda
- 1 tsp cinnamon
- 1 cup blueberries

DIRECTIONS

1. In a bowl combine all dry ingredients
2. In another bowl combine all dry ingredients
3. Combine wet and dry ingredients together
4. Fold in blueberries and mix well
5. Pour mixture into 8-12 prepared muffin cups, fill 2/3 of the cups
6. Bake for 18-20 minutes at 375 F

7. **When ready remove from the oven and serve**

PAPAYA MUFFINS

Serves: *8-12*

Prep Time: *10* Minutes

Cook Time: *20* Minutes

Total Time: *30* Minutes

INGREDIENTS

- 2 eggs
- 1 tablespoon olive oil
- 1 cup milk
- 2 cups whole wheat flour
- 1 tsp baking soda
- ¼ tsp baking soda
- 1 tsp cinnamon
- 1 cup papaya

DIRECTIONS

1. In a bowl combine all dry ingredients
2. In another bowl combine all dry ingredients
3. Combine wet and dry ingredients together
4. Pour mixture into 8-12 prepared muffin cups, fill 2/3 of the cups
5. Bake for 18-20 minutes at 375 F
6. When ready remove from the oven and serve

CORN OMELETTE

Serves: *1*

Prep Time: *5* Minutes

Cook Time: *10* Minutes

Total Time: *15* Minutes

INGREDIENTS

- 2 eggs
- ¼ tsp salt
- ¼ tsp black pepper
- 1 tablespoon olive oil
- ¼ cup cheese
- ¼ tsp basil
- 1 cup corn

DIRECTIONS

1. In a bowl combine all ingredients together and mix well
2. In a skillet heat olive oil and pour the egg mixture
3. Cook for 1-2 minutes per side
4. When ready remove omelette from the skillet and serve

MUSHROOM OMELETTE

Serves: *1*

Prep Time: *5* Minutes

Cook Time: *10* Minutes

Total Time: *15* Minutes

INGREDIENTS

- 2 eggs
- ¼ tsp salt
- ¼ tsp black pepper
- 1 tablespoon olive oil
- ¼ cup cheese
- ¼ tsp basil
- 1 cup mushrooms

DIRECTIONS

1. In a bowl combine all ingredients together and mix well
2. In a skillet heat olive oil and pour the egg mixture
3. Cook for 1-2 minutes per side
4. When ready remove omelette from the skillet and serve

YAMS OMELETTE

Serves: *1*

Prep Time: *5* Minutes

Cook Time: *10* Minutes

Total Time: *15* Minutes

INGREDIENTS

- 2 eggs
- ¼ tsp salt
- ¼ tsp black pepper
- 1 tablespoon olive oil
- ¼ cup cheese
- ¼ tsp basil
- 1 cup yams

DIRECTIONS

1. In a bowl combine all ingredients together and mix well
2. In a skillet heat olive oil and pour the egg mixture
3. Cook for 1-2 minutes per side
4. When ready remove omelette from the skillet and serve

RAISIN BREAKFAST MIX

Serves: *1*
Prep Time: *5* Minutes

Cook Time: *5* Minutes

Total Time: *10* Minutes

INGREDIENTS

- **½ cup dried raisins**
- **½ cup dried pecans**
- **¼ cup almonds**
- **1 cup coconut milk**
- **1 tsp cinnamon**

DIRECTIONS

1. **In a bowl combine all ingredients together**
2. **Serve with milk**

SAUSAGE BREAKFAST SANDWICH

Serves: 2
Prep Time: *5* Minutes

Cook Time: *15* Minutes

Total Time: *20* Minutes

INGREDIENTS

- ¼ cup egg substitute
- 1 muffin
- 1 turkey sausage patty
- 1 tablespoon cheddar cheese

DIRECTIONS

1. In a skillet pour egg and cook on low heat
2. Place turkey sausage patty in a pan and cook for 4-5 minutes per side
3. On a toasted muffin place the cooked egg, top with a sausage patty and cheddar cheese
4. Serve when ready

STRAWBERRY MUFFINS

Serves: *8-12*
Prep Time: ***10*** Minutes

Cook Time: ***20*** Minutes

Total Time: ***30*** Minutes

INGREDIENTS

- 2 eggs
- 1 tablespoon olive oil
- 1 cup milk
- 2 cups whole wheat flour
- 1 tsp baking soda
- ¼ tsp baking soda
- 1 tsp cinnamon
- 1 cup strawberries

DIRECTIONS

1. **In a bowl combine all dry ingredients**
2. **In another bowl combine all dry ingredients**
3. **Combine wet and dry ingredients together**
4. **Pour mixture into 8-12 prepared muffin cups, fill 2/3 of the cups**
5. **Bake for 18-20 minutes at 375 F**
6. **When ready remove from the oven and serve**

LEEK FRITATTA

Serves: 2

Prep Time: *10* Minutes

Cook Time: *20* Minutes

Total Time: *30* Minutes

INGREDIENTS

- ½ lb. leek
- 1 tablespoon olive oil
- ½ red onion
- ¼ tsp salt
- 2 ggs
- 2 oz. cheddar cheese
- 1 garlic clove
- ¼ tsp dill

DIRECTIONS

1. In a bowl whisk eggs with salt and cheese
2. In a frying pan heat olive oil and pour egg mixture
3. Add remaining ingredients and mix well
4. Serve when ready

KALE FRITATTA

Serves: 2

Prep Time: *10* Minutes

Cook Time: *20* Minutes

Total Time: *30* Minutes

INGREDIENTS

- 1 cup kale
- 1 tablespoon olive oil
- ½ red onion
- ¼ tsp salt
- 2 eggs
- 2 oz. cheddar cheese
- 1 garlic clove
- ¼ tsp dill

DIRECTIONS

1. In a skillet sauté kale until tender
2. In a bowl whisk eggs with salt and cheese
3. In a frying pan heat olive oil and pour egg mixture
4. Add remaining ingredients and mix well
5. Serve when ready

GREENS FRITATTA

Serves: 2

Prep Time: *10* Minutes

Cook Time: *20* Minutes

Total Time: *30* Minutes

INGREDIENTS

- **½ lb. greens**
- **1 tablespoon olive oil**
- **½ red onion**
- **¼ tsp salt**
- **2 eggs**
- **2 oz. parmesan cheese**
- **1 garlic clove**
- **¼ tsp dill**

DIRECTIONS

1. **In a bowl whisk eggs with salt and parmesan cheese**
2. **In a frying pan heat olive oil and pour egg mixture**
3. **Add remaining ingredients and mix well**
4. **Serve when ready**

BROCCOLI FRITATTA

Serves: 2

Prep Time: *10* Minutes

Cook Time: *20* Minutes

Total Time: *30* Minutes

INGREDIENTS

- 1 cup broccoli
- 1 tablespoon olive oil
- ½ red onion
- ¼ tsp salt
- 2 oz. cheddar cheese
- 1 garlic clove
- ¼ tsp dill

DIRECTIONS

1. In a skillet sauté broccoli until tender
2. In a bowl whisk eggs with salt and cheese
3. In a frying pan heat olive oil and pour egg mixture
4. Add remaining ingredients and mix well
5. When ready serve with sautéed broccoli

DESSERTS

BREAKFAST COOKIES

Serves: *8-12*
Prep Time: *5* Minutes

Cook Time: *15* Minutes

Total Time: *20* Minutes

INGREDIENTS

- **1 cup rolled oats**
- **¼ cup applesauce**
- **½ tsp vanilla extract**
- **3 tablespoons chocolate chips**
- **2 tablespoons dried fruits**
- **1 tsp cinnamon**

DIRECTIONS

1. **Preheat the oven to 325 F**
2. **In a bowl combine all ingredients together and mix well**

3. Scoop cookies using an ice cream scoop
4. Place cookies onto a prepared baking sheet
5. Place in the oven for 12-15 minutes or until the cookies are done
6. When ready remove from the oven and serve

BLUEBERRY PIE

Serves: *8-12*
Prep Time: *15* Minutes

Cook Time: *35* Minutes

Total Time: *50* Minutes

INGREDIENTS

- **pastry sheets**
- **¼ tsp lavender**
- **1 cup brown sugar**
- **4-5 cups blueberries**
- **1 tablespoon lemon juice**
- **1 cup almonds**
- **2 tablespoons butter**

DIRECTIONS

1. **Line a pie plate or pie form with pastry and cover the edges of the plate depending on your preference**
2. **In a bowl combine all pie ingredients together and mix well**
3. **Pour the mixture over the pastry**
4. **Bake at 400-425 F for 25-30 minutes or until golden brown**
5. **When ready remove from the oven and let it rest for 15 minutes**

PUMPKIN PIE

Serves: *8-12*
Prep Time: *15* Minutes

Cook Time: *35* Minutes

Total Time: *50* Minutes

INGREDIENTS

- pastry sheets
- 1 cup buttermilk
- 1 can pumpkin
- 1 cup sugar
- 1 tsp cinnamon
- 1 tsp vanilla extract
- 2 eggs

DIRECTIONS

1. Line a pie plate or pie form with pastry and cover the edges of the plate depending on your preference
2. In a bowl combine all pie ingredients together and mix well
3. Pour the mixture over the pastry
4. Bake at 400-425 F for 25-30 minutes or until golden brown
5. When ready remove from the oven and let it rest for 15 minutes

RICOTTA ICE-CREAM

Serves: *6-8*

Prep Time: *15* Minutes

Cook Time: *15* Minutes

Total Time: *30* Minutes

INGREDIENTS

- 1 cup almonds
- 1-pint vanilla ice cream
- 2 cups ricotta cheese
- 1 cup honey

DIRECTIONS

1. In a saucepan whisk together all ingredients
2. Mix until bubbly
3. Strain into a bowl and cool
4. Whisk in favorite fruits and mix well
5. Cover and refrigerate for 2-3 hours
6. Pour mixture in the ice-cream maker and follow manufacturer instructions
7. Serve when ready

SAFFRON ICE-CREAM

Serves: *6-8*

Prep Time: *15* Minutes

Cook Time: *15* Minutes

Total Time: *30* Minutes

INGREDIENTS

- 4 egg yolks
- 1 cup heavy cream
- 1 cup milk
- ½ cup brown sugar
- 1 tsp saffron
- 1 tsp vanilla extract

DIRECTIONS

1. In a saucepan whisk together all ingredients
2. Mix until bubbly
3. Strain into a bowl and cool
4. Whisk in favorite fruits and mix well
5. Cover and refrigerate for 2-3 hours
6. Pour mixture in the ice-cream maker and follow manufacturer instructions
7. Serve when ready

TURMERIC-MANGO SMOOTHIE

Serves: *1*
Prep Time: *5* Minutes

Cook Time: *5* Minutes

Total Time: ***10*** Minutes

INGREDIENTS

- **1 cup Greek yogurt**
- **¼ cup orange juice**
- **1 banana**
- **1 tablespoon turmeric**
- **1 tsp vanilla extract**
- **1 cup ice**

DIRECTIONS

1. **In a blender place all ingredients and blend until smooth**
2. **Pour smoothie in a glass and serve**

AVOCADO-KALE SMOOTHIE

Serves: *1*
Prep Time: *5* Minutes

Cook Time: *5* Minutes

Total Time: ***10*** Minutes

INGREDIENTS

- 1 cup coconut milk
- 1 tablespoon lemon juice
- 1 bunch kale
- 1 cup spinach
- ¼ avocado
- 1 cup ice

DIRECTIONS

1. **In a blender place all ingredients and blend until smooth**
2. **Pour smoothie in a glass and serve**

BUTTERMILK SMOOTHIE

Serves: *1*

Prep Time: *5* Minutes

Cook Time: *5* Minutes

Total Time: ***10*** Minutes

INGREDIENTS

- **1 cup ice**
- **1 cup strawberries**
- **1 cup blueberries**
- **1 cup buttermilk**
- **½ tsp vanilla extract**

DIRECTIONS

1. **In a blender place all ingredients and blend until smooth**
2. **Pour smoothie in a glass and serve**

GREEN SMOOTHIE

Serves: *1*

Prep Time: *5* Minutes

Cook Time: *5* Minutes

Total Time: ***10*** Minutes

INGREDIENTS

- **1 cup berries**
- **1 cup baby spinach**
- **1 tablespoon orange juice**
- **¼ cup coconut water**
- **½ cup Greek yogurt**

DIRECTIONS

1. **In a blender place all ingredients and blend until smooth**
2. **Pour smoothie in a glass and serve**

FRUIT SMOOTHIE

Serves: *1*

Prep Time: *5* Minutes

Cook Time: *5* Minutes

Total Time: *10* Minutes

INGREDIENTS

- 1 mango
- 1 cup vanilla yogurt
- 2 tablespoons honey
- 1 tablespoon lime juice
- 1 banana
- 1 can strawberries
- 1 kiwi

DIRECTIONS

1. In a blender place all ingredients and blend until smooth
2. Pour smoothie in a glass and serve

MANGO SMOOTHIE

Serves: *1*
Prep Time: *5* Minutes

Cook Time: *5* Minutes

Total Time: *10* Minutes

INGREDIENTS

- **2 cups mango**
- **1 cup buttermilk**
- **1 tsp vanilla extract**
- **1 cup kiwi**
- **½ cup coconut milk**

DIRECTIONS

1. **In a blender place all ingredients and blend until smooth**
2. **Pour smoothie in a glass and serve**

DREAMSICLE SMOOTHIE

Serves: *1*

Prep Time: *5* Minutes

Cook Time: *5* Minutes

Total Time: ***10*** Minutes

INGREDIENTS

- **1 cup Greek yogurt**
- **1 cup ice**
- **¼ cup mango**
- **1 orange**
- **1 pinch cinnamon**

DIRECTIONS

1. **In a blender place all ingredients and blend until smooth**
2. **Pour smoothie in a glass and serve**

FIG SMOOTHIE

Serves: *1*

Prep Time: *5* Minutes

Cook Time: *5* Minutes

Total Time: *10* Minutes

INGREDIENTS

- **1 cup ice**
- **1 cup vanilla yogurt**
- **1 cup coconut milk**
- **1 tsp honey**
- **4 figs**

DIRECTIONS

1. **In a blender place all ingredients and blend until smooth**
2. **Pour smoothie in a glass and serve**

POMEGRANATE SMOOTHIE

Serves: *1*

Prep Time: *5* Minutes

Cook Time: *5* Minutes

Total Time: *10* Minutes

INGREDIENTS

- **2 cups blueberries**
- **1 cup pomegranate**
- **1 tablespoon honey**
- **1 cup Greek yogurt**

DIRECTIONS

1. **In a blender place all ingredients and blend until smooth**
2. **Pour smoothie in a glass and serve**

GINGER-KALE SMOOTHIE

Serves:	*1*	
Prep Time:	*5*	Minutes
Cook Time:	*5*	Minutes
Total Time:	*10*	Minutes

INGREDIENTS

- 1 cup kale
- 1 banana
- 1 cup almond milk
- 1 cup vanilla yogurt
- 1 tsp chia seeds
- ¼ tsp ginger

DIRECTIONS

1. **In a blender place all ingredients and blend until smooth**
2. **Pour smoothie in a glass and serve**

THIRD COOKBOOK

PINEAPPLE PANCAKES

Serves: *4*

Prep Time: *10* Minutes

Cook Time: *20* Minutes

Total Time: *30* Minutes

INGREDIENTS

- **1 cup whole wheat flour**
- **¼ tsp baking soda**
- **¼ tsp baking powder**
- **1 cup pineapple**
- **2 eggs**
- **1 cup milk**

DIRECTIONS

1. **In a bowl combine all ingredients together and mix well**
2. **In a skillet heat olive oil**
3. **Pour ¼ of the batter and cook each pancake for 1-2 minutes per side**
4. **When ready remove from heat and serve**

ALMOND PANCAKES

Serves: *4*

Prep Time: *10* Minutes

Cook Time: *30* Minutes

Total Time: *40* Minutes

INGREDIENTS

- 1 cup whole wheat flour
- ¼ tsp baking soda
- ¼ tsp baking powder
- 1 cup almonds
- 2 eggs
- 1 cup milk

DIRECTIONS

1. In a bowl combine all ingredients together and mix well
2. In a skillet heat olive oil
3. Pour ¼ of the batter and cook each pancake for 1-2 minutes per side
4. When ready remove from heat and serve

APPLE PANCAKES

Serves: *4*

Prep Time: *10* Minutes

Cook Time: *20* Minutes

Total Time: *30* Minutes

INGREDIENTS

- 1 cup whole wheat flour
- ¼ tsp baking soda
- ¼ tsp baking powder
- 1 cup mashed apple
- 2 eggs
- 1 cup milk

DIRECTIONS

5. In a bowl combine all ingredients together and mix well
6. In a skillet heat olive oil
7. Pour ¼ of the batter and cook each pancake for 1-2 minutes per side
8. When ready remove from heat and serve

STRAWBERRY PANCAKES

Serves: ***4***

Prep Time: ***10*** Minutes

Cook Time: ***20*** Minutes

Total Time: ***30*** Minutes

INGREDIENTS

- **1 cup whole wheat flour**
- **¼ tsp baking soda**
- **¼ tsp baking powder**
- **1 cup strawberries**
- **2 eggs**
- **1 cup milk**

DIRECTIONS

1. **In a bowl combine all ingredients together and mix well**
2. **In a skillet heat olive oil**
3. **Pour ¼ of the batter and cook each pancake for 1-2 minutes per side**
4. **When ready remove from heat and serve**

PEAR PANCAKES

Serves: *4*
Prep Time: *10* Minutes

Cook Time: *30* Minutes

Total Time: *40* Minutes

INGREDIENTS

- 1 cup whole wheat flour
- ¼ tsp baking soda
- ¼ tsp baking powder
- 2 eggs
- 1 cup milk
- 1 cup mashed pear

DIRECTIONS

1. In a bowl combine all ingredients together and mix well
2. In a skillet heat olive oil
3. Pour ¼ of the batter and cook each pancake for 1-2 minutes per side
4. When ready remove from heat and serve

LETTUCE OMELETTE

Serves: *1*

Prep Time: *5* Minutes

Cook Time: *10* Minutes

Total Time: *15* Minutes

INGREDIENTS

- **2 eggs**
- **¼ tsp salt**
- **¼ tsp black pepper**
- **1 tablespoon olive oil**
- **¼ cup cheese**
- **¼ tsp basil**
- **1 bunch lettuce**

DIRECTIONS

1. **In a bowl combine all ingredients together and mix well**
2. **In a skillet heat olive oil and pour the egg mixture**
3. **Cook for 1-2 minutes per side**
4. **When ready remove omelette from the skillet and serve**

ZUCCHINI OMELETTE

Serves: *1*

Prep Time: *5* Minutes

Cook Time: *10* Minutes

Total Time: *15* Minutes

INGREDIENTS

- 2 eggs
- ¼ tsp salt
- ¼ tsp black pepper
- 1 tablespoon olive oil
- ¼ cup cheese
- ¼ tsp basil
- 1 cup zucchini

DIRECTIONS

1. **In a bowl combine all ingredients together and mix well**
2. **In a skillet heat olive oil and pour the egg mixture**
3. **Cook for 1-2 minutes per side**
4. **When ready remove omelette from the skillet and serve**

JICAMA OMELETTE

Serves: *1*

Prep Time: *5* Minutes

Cook Time: *10* Minutes

Total Time: *15* Minutes

INGREDIENTS

- **2 eggs**
- **¼ tsp salt**
- **¼ tsp black pepper**
- **1 tablespoon olive oil**
- **¼ cup cheese**
- **¼ tsp basil**
- **½ cup jicama**
- **1 cup red onion**

DIRECTIONS

1. **In a bowl combine all ingredients together and mix well**
2. **In a skillet heat olive oil and pour the egg mixture**
3. **Cook for 1-2 minutes per side**
4. **When ready remove omelette from the skillet and serve**

MUSHROOM OMELETTE

Serves: *1*

Prep Time: *5* Minutes

Cook Time: *10* Minutes

Total Time: *15* Minutes

INGREDIENTS

- 2 eggs
- ¼ tsp salt
- ¼ tsp black pepper
- 1 tablespoon olive oil
- ¼ cup cheese
- ¼ tsp basil
- 1 cup mushrooms

DIRECTIONS

1. **In a bowl combine all ingredients together and mix well**
2. **In a skillet heat olive oil and pour the egg mixture**
3. **Cook for 1-2 minutes per side**
4. **When ready remove omelette from the skillet and serve**

BASIL OMELETTE

Serves: *1*
Prep Time: *5* Minutes

Cook Time: *10* Minutes

Total Time: *15* Minutes

INGREDIENTS

- 2 eggs
- ¼ tsp salt
- ¼ tsp black pepper
- 1 tablespoon olive oil
- ¼ cup cheese
- ¼ tsp basil
- 1 cup tomatoes

DIRECTIONS

1. In a bowl combine all ingredients together and mix well
2. In a skillet heat olive oil and pour the egg mixture
3. Cook for 1-2 minutes per side
4. When ready remove omelette from the skillet and serve

MUSHROOM OMELETTE

Serves: *1*
Prep Time: *5* Minutes

Cook Time: *10* Minutes

Total Time: *15* Minutes

INGREDIENTS

- **2 eggs**
- **¼ tsp salt**
- **¼ tsp black pepper**
- **1 tablespoon olive oil**
- **¼ cup cheese**
- **¼ tsp basil**
- **1 cup mushrooms**

DIRECTIONS

1. **In a bowl combine all ingredients together and mix well**
2. **In a skillet heat olive oil and pour the egg mixture**
3. **Cook for 1-2 minutes per side**
4. **When ready remove omelette from the skillet and serve**

BREAKFAST MIX

Serves: *1*

Prep Time: *5* Minutes

Cook Time: *5* Minutes

Total Time: *10* Minutes

INGREDIENTS

- **1 cup corn cereal**
- **1 cup rice cereal**
- **¼ cup cocoa cereal**
- **¼ cup rice cakes**

DIRECTIONS

1. **In a bowl combine all ingredients together**
2. **Serve with milk**

SAUSAGE BREAKFAST SANDWICH

Serves: 2
Prep Time: *5* Minutes

Cook Time: *15* Minutes

Total Time: *20* Minutes

INGREDIENTS

- ¼ cup egg substitute
- 1 muffin
- 1 turkey sausage patty
- 1 tablespoon cheddar cheese

DIRECTIONS

1. **In a skillet pour egg and cook on low heat**
2. **Place turkey sausage patty in a pan and cook for 4-5 minutes per side**
3. **On a toasted muffin place the cooked egg, top with a sausage patty and cheddar cheese**
4. **Serve when ready**

BREAKFAST GRANOLA

Serves: 2
Prep Time: 5 Minutes

Cook Time: *30* Minutes

Total Time: *35* Minutes

INGREDIENTS

- 1 tsp vanilla extract
- 1 tablespoon honey
- 1 lb. rolled oats
- 2 tablespoons sesame seeds
- ¼ lb. almonds
- ¼ lb. berries

DIRECTIONS

1. Preheat the oven to 325 F
2. Spread the granola onto a baking sheet
3. Bake for 12-15 minutes, remove and mix everything
4. Bake for another 12-15 minutes or until slightly brown
5. When ready remove from the oven and serve

PANCAKES

BANANA PANCAKES

Serves: *4*

Prep Time: *10* Minutes

Cook Time: *20* Minutes

Total Time: *30* Minutes

INGREDIENTS

- 1 cup whole wheat flour
- ¼ tsp baking soda
- ¼ tsp baking powder
- 1 cup mashed banana
- 2 eggs
- 1 cup milk

DIRECTIONS

1. In a bowl combine all ingredients together and mix well
2. In a skillet heat olive oil
3. Pour ¼ of the batter and cook each pancake for 1-2 minutes per side
4. When ready remove from heat and serve

PINEAPPLE PANCAKES

Serves: *4*
Prep Time: *10* Minutes
Cook Time: *20* Minutes
Total Time: *30* Minutes

INGREDIENTS

- **1 cup whole wheat flour**
- **¼ tsp baking soda**
- **¼ tsp baking powder**
- **1 cup pineapple**
- **2 eggs**
- **1 cup milk**

DIRECTIONS

1. **In a bowl combine all ingredients together and mix well**
2. **In a skillet heat olive oil**
3. **Pour ¼ of the batter and cook each pancake for 1-2 minutes per side**
4. **When ready remove from heat and serve**

ALMOND PANCAKES

Serves: *4*

Prep Time: *10* Minutes

Cook Time: *30* Minutes

Total Time: *40* Minutes

INGREDIENTS

- 1 cup whole wheat flour
- ¼ tsp baking soda
- ¼ tsp baking powder
- 1 cup almonds
- 2 eggs
- 1 cup milk

DIRECTIONS

1. In a bowl combine all ingredients together and mix well
2. In a skillet heat olive oil
3. Pour ¼ of the batter and cook each pancake for 1-2 minutes per side
4. When ready remove from heat and serve

APPLE PANCAKES

Serves: *4*
Prep Time: *10* Minutes

Cook Time: *20* Minutes

Total Time: *30* Minutes

INGREDIENTS

- **1 cup whole wheat flour**
- **¼ tsp baking soda**
- **¼ tsp baking powder**
- **1 cup mashed apple**
- **2 eggs**
- **1 cup milk**

DIRECTIONS

1. **In a bowl combine all ingredients together and mix well**
2. **In a skillet heat olive oil**
3. **Pour ¼ of the batter and cook each pancake for 1-2 minutes per side**
4. **When ready remove from heat and serve**

STRAWBERRY PANCAKES

Serves: ***4***

Prep Time: ***10*** Minutes

Cook Time: ***20*** Minutes

Total Time: ***30*** Minutes

INGREDIENTS

- 1 cup whole wheat flour
- ¼ tsp baking soda
- ¼ tsp baking powder
- 1 cup strawberries
- 2 eggs
- 1 cup milk

DIRECTIONS

1. In a bowl combine all ingredients together and mix well
2. In a skillet heat olive oil
3. Pour ¼ of the batter and cook each pancake for 1-2 minutes per side
4. When ready remove from heat and serve

PEAR PANCAKES

Serves: *4*

Prep Time: *10* Minutes

Cook Time: *30* Minutes

Total Time: *40* Minutes

INGREDIENTS

- **1 cup whole wheat flour**
- **¼ tsp baking soda**
- **¼ tsp baking powder**
- **2 eggs**
- **1 cup milk**
- **1 cup mashed pear**

DIRECTIONS

1. **In a bowl combine all ingredients together and mix well**
2. **In a skillet heat olive oil**
3. **Pour ¼ of the batter and cook each pancake for 1-2 minutes per side**
4. **When ready remove from heat and serve**

COOKIES

BREAKFAST COOKIES

Serves: *8-12*

Prep Time: *5* Minutes

Cook Time: *15* Minutes

Total Time: *20* Minutes

INGREDIENTS

- **1 cup rolled oats**
- **¼ cup applesauce**
- **½ tsp vanilla extract**
- **3 tablespoons chocolate chips**
- **2 tablespoons dried fruits**
- **1 tsp cinnamon**

DIRECTIONS

1. **Preheat the oven to 325 F**
2. **In a bowl combine all ingredients together and mix well**
3. **Scoop cookies using an ice cream scoop**
4. **Place cookies onto a prepared baking sheet**
5. **Place in the oven for 12-15 minutes or until the cookies are done**
6. **When ready remove from the oven and serve**

SMOOOTHIES

FIG SMOOTHIE

Serves: *1*
Prep Time: *5* Minutes

Cook Time: *5* Minutes

Total Time: ***10*** Minutes

INGREDIENTS

- **1 cup ice**
- **1 cup vanilla yogurt**
- **1 cup coconut milk**
- **1 tsp honey**
- **4 figs**

DIRECTIONS

1. **In a blender place all ingredients and blend until smooth**
2. **Pour smoothie in a glass and serve**

POMEGRANATE SMOOTHIE

Serves: *1*

Prep Time: *5* Minutes

Cook Time: *5* Minutes

Total Time: *10* Minutes

INGREDIENTS

- **2 cups blueberries**
- **1 cup pomegranate**
- **1 tablespoon honey**
- **1 cup Greek yogurt**

DIRECTIONS

1. **In a blender place all ingredients and blend until smooth**
2. **Pour smoothie in a glass and serve**

GINGER-KALE SMOOTHIE

Serves: *1*
Prep Time: *5* Minutes

Cook Time: *5* Minutes

Total Time: ***10*** Minutes

INGREDIENTS

- **1 cup kale**
- **1 banana**
- **1 cup almond milk**
- **1 cup vanilla yogurt**
- **1 tsp chia seeds**
- **¼ tsp ginger**

DIRECTIONS

1. **In a blender place all ingredients and blend until smooth**
2. **Pour smoothie in a glass and serve**

BERRY YOGHURT SMOOTHIE

Serves: *1*
Prep Time: *5* Minutes
Cook Time: *5* Minutes
Total Time: ***10*** Minutes

INGREDIENTS

- 6 oz. berries
- 2 bananas
- 4 oz. vanilla yoghurt
- 1 cup milk
- 1 tablespoon honey

DIRECTIONS

1. **In a blender place all ingredients and blend until smooth**
2. **Pour smoothie in a glass and serve**

COCONUT SMOOTHIE

Serves: *1*

Prep Time: *5* Minutes

Cook Time: *5* Minutes

Total Time: *10* Minutes

INGREDIENTS

- **2 mangoes**
- **2 bananas**
- **1 cup coconut water**
- **1 cup ice**
- **1 tablespoon honey**
- **1 cup Greek Yoghurt**
- **1 cup strawberries**

DIRECTIONS

1. **In a blender place all ingredients and blend until smooth**
2. **Pour smoothie in a glass and serve**

RASPBERRY-VANILLA SMOOTHIE

Serves: *1*

Prep Time: *5* Minutes

Cook Time: *5* Minutes

Total Time: ***10*** Minutes

INGREDIENTS

- ¼ cup sugar
- ¼ cup water
- 1 cup Greek yoghurt
- 1 cup raspberries
- 1 tsp vanilla extract
- 1 cup ice

DIRECTIONS

1. **In a blender place all ingredients and blend until smooth**
2. **Pour smoothie in a glass and serve**

CHERRY SMOOTHIE

Serves: *1*

Prep Time: *5* Minutes

Cook Time: *5* Minutes

Total Time: *10* Minutes

INGREDIENTS

- 1 can cherries
- 2 tablespoons peanut butter
- 1 tablespoon honey
- 1 cup Greek Yoghurt
- 1 cup coconut milk

DIRECTIONS

1. In a blender place all ingredients and blend until smooth
2. Pour smoothie in a glass and serve

CHOCOLATE SMOOTHIE

Serves: *1*
Prep Time: *5* Minutes

Cook Time: *5* Minutes

Total Time: ***10*** Minutes

INGREDIENTS

- **2 bananas**
- **1 cup Greek Yoghurt**
- **1 tablespoon honey**
- **1 tablespoon cocoa powder**
- **½ cup chocolate chips**
- **¼ cup almond milk**

DIRECTIONS

1. **In a blender place all ingredients and blend until smooth**
2. **Pour smoothie in a glass and serve**

TOFU SMOOTHIE

Serves: *1*

Prep Time: *5* Minutes

Cook Time: *5* Minutes

Total Time: ***10*** Minutes

INGREDIENTS

- **1 cup blueberries**
- **¼ cup tofu**
- **¼ cup pomegranate juice**
- **1 cup ice**
- **½ cup agave nectar**

DIRECTIONS

1. **In a blender place all ingredients and blend until smooth**
2. **Pour smoothie in a glass and serve**

ORANGE SMOOTHIE

Serves: *1*

Prep Time: *5* Minutes

Cook Time: *5* Minutes

Total Time: *10* Minutes

INGREDIENTS

- 1 orange
- ½ cup orange juice
- ½ banana
- 1 tsp vanilla essence

DIRECTIONS

1. **In a blender place all ingredients and blend until smooth**
2. **Pour smoothie in a glass and serve**

RAISIN DATE SMOOTHIE

Serves: *1*

Prep Time: *5* Minutes

Cook Time: *5* Minutes

Total Time: *10* Minutes

INGREDIENTS

- **¼ cup raisins**
- **2 Medjool dates**
- **1 cup berries**
- **1 cup almond milk**
- **1 tsp chia seeds**

DIRECTIONS

1. **In a blender place all ingredients and blend until smooth**
2. **Pour smoothie in a glass and serve**

MUFFINS

SIMPLE MUFFINS

Serves: *8-12*
Prep Time: *10* Minutes

Cook Time: *20* Minutes

Total Time: *30* Minutes

INGREDIENTS

- 2 eggs
- 1 tablespoon olive oil
- 1 cup milk
- 2 cups whole wheat flour
- 1 tsp baking soda
- ¼ tsp baking soda
- 1 cup pumpkin puree
- 1 tsp cinnamon
- ¼ cup molasses

DIRECTIONS

1. In a bowl combine all wet ingredients
2. In another bowl combine all dry ingredients
3. Combine wet and dry ingredients together
4. Pour mixture into 8-12 prepared muffin cups, fill 2/3 of the cups

5. **Bake for 18-20 minutes at 375 F**
6. **When ready remove from the oven and serve**

GINGERBREAD MUFFINS

Serves: *8-12*
Prep Time: ***10*** Minutes

Cook Time: ***20*** Minutes

Total Time: ***30*** Minutes

INGREDIENTS

- 2 eggs
- 1 tablespoon olive oil
- 1 cup milk
- 2 cups whole wheat flour
- 1 tsp baking soda
- ¼ tsp baking soda
- 1 tsp ginger
- 1 tsp cinnamon
- ¼ cup molasses

DIRECTIONS

1. **In a bowl combine all wet ingredients**
2. **In another bowl combine all dry ingredients**
3. **Combine wet and dry ingredients together**
4. **Fold in ginger and mix well**
5. **Pour mixture into 8-12 prepared muffin cups, fill 2/3 of the cups**

6. **Bake for 18-20 minutes at 375 F**
7. **When ready remove from the oven and serve**

CHERRIES MUFFINS

Serves: *8-12*

Prep Time: *10* Minutes

Cook Time: *20* Minutes

Total Time: *30* Minutes

INGREDIENTS

- 2 eggs
- 1 tablespoon olive oil
- 1 cup milk
- 2 cups whole wheat flour
- 1 tsp baking soda
- ¼ tsp baking soda
- 1 tsp cinnamon
- 1 cup mashed cherries

DIRECTIONS

1. In a bowl combine all wet ingredients
2. In another bowl combine all dry ingredients
3. Combine wet and dry ingredients together
4. Pour mixture into 8-12 prepared muffin cups, fill 2/3 of the cups
5. Bake for 18-20 minutes at 375 F
6. When ready remove from the oven and serve

BLUEBERRY MUFFINS

Serves: *8-12*

Prep Time: ***10*** Minutes

Cook Time: ***20*** Minutes

Total Time: ***30*** Minutes

INGREDIENTS

- 2 eggs
- 1 tablespoon olive oil
- 1 cup milk
- 2 cups whole wheat flour
- 1 tsp baking soda
- ¼ tsp baking soda
- 1 tsp cinnamon
- 1 cup blueberries

DIRECTIONS

1. In a bowl combine all wet ingredients
2. In another bowl combine all dry ingredients
3. Combine wet and dry ingredients together
4. Fold in blueberries and mix well
5. Pour mixture into 8-12 prepared muffin cups, fill 2/3 of the cups
6. Bake for 18-20 minutes at 375 F

BERRIES MUFFINS

Serves: *8-12*

Prep Time: *10* Minutes

Cook Time: *20* Minutes

Total Time: *30* Minutes

INGREDIENTS

- 2 eggs
- 1 tablespoon olive oil
- 1 cup milk
- 2 cups whole wheat flour
- 1 tsp baking soda
- ¼ tsp baking soda
- 1 tsp cinnamon
- 1 cup berries

DIRECTIONS

1. In a bowl combine all wet ingredients
2. In another bowl combine all dry ingredients
3. Combine wet and dry ingredients together
4. Pour mixture into 8-12 prepared muffin cups, fill 2/3 of the cups
5. Bake for 18-20 minutes at 375 F
6. When ready remove from the oven and serve

CHOCOLATE MUFFINS

Serves: *8-12*

Prep Time: *10* Minutes

Cook Time: *20* Minutes

Total Time: *30* Minutes

INGREDIENTS

- **2 eggs**
- **1 tablespoon olive oil**
- **1 cup milk**
- **2 cups whole wheat flour**
- **1 tsp baking soda**
- **¼ tsp baking soda**
- **1 tsp cinnamon**
- **1 cup chocolate chips**

DIRECTIONS

1. **In a bowl combine all wet ingredients**
2. **In another bowl combine all dry ingredients**
3. **Combine wet and dry ingredients together**
4. **Fold in chocolate chips and mix well**
5. **Pour mixture into 8-12 prepared muffin cups, fill 2/3 of the cups**
6. **Bake for 18-20 minutes at 375 F**

RASPBERRIES MUFFINS

Serves: *8-12*

Prep Time: ***10*** Minutes

Cook Time: ***20*** Minutes

Total Time: ***30*** Minutes

INGREDIENTS

- 2 eggs
- 1 tablespoon olive oil
- 1 cup milk
- 2 cups whole wheat flour
- 1 tsp baking soda
- ¼ tsp baking soda
- 1 tsp cinnamon
- 1 cup raspberries

DIRECTIONS

1. In a bowl combine all wet ingredients
2. In another bowl combine all dry ingredients
3. Combine wet and dry ingredients together
4. Pour mixture into 8-12 prepared muffin cups, fill 2/3 of the cups
5. Bake for 18-20 minutes at 375 F
6. When ready remove from the oven and serve

THANK YOU FOR READING THIS BOOK!